Finches as Pets

The Complete Owner's Guide

Includes Information on the House Finch, Zebra Finch,
Gouldian Finch, Red, Yellow, Purple, Green, and Goldfinch,
Breeding, Feeding and Cages

Foreword

Finches come in a wide variety of colors and patterns – they are also very social and friendly birds which makes them a joy to keep as pets. If you have ever thought about keeping finches, or if you are just curious to learn more about them, this is the right book for you. In this book you will find a wealth of knowledge about finches – including tips for keeping them as pets – so you can determine whether these beautiful little birds are the right pet for you.

Acknowledgements

I would like to extend my sincerest thanks to my family for their endless support as I worked through this book.

Special thanks to my wife who has always encouraged my love for these wonderful birds and who gave me the idea to write this book.

Table of Contents

Chapter One: Introduction

When you think about pet birds, what comes to mind? Perhaps you think of a giant cockatoo with a feathery plume or a noisy macaw that never seems to sleep. If these are the only pet birds you can think of, you are missing out! Countless bird enthusiasts have discovered the joy of keeping finches as pets. Finches come in a wide variety of colors and patterns and they are much smaller and easier to keep than cockatoos, parrots, and macaws. If you have ever considered keeping finches as pets, or if you are simply curious to learn more, this book is the perfect place to start!

Finches are a very social group of birds that need to be kept in pairs or groups. When properly cared for, finches can be very friendly and they are often prolific breeders, even in captivity. Within the pages of this book you will find a wealth of information about finches including detailed instructions for keeping them as pets. You will learn about various finch species including the popular zebra finch, house finch, and Gouldian finch – you will also learn about the many colors of finches.

By the time you finish this book you will be equipped with enough knowledge to know whether finches are the right pet for you and you will have the foundation you need to get started in owning and caring for these wonderful birds. So what are you waiting for? Keep reading!

Glossary of Important Terms

Arboreal – Referring to a tree-dwelling animal.

Avian – Pertaining to birds.

Axillars – The feathers located on the underside at the base of a bird's wing.

Beak – The mouth of a bird consisting of the upper and lower mandibles.

Breast – The chest of a bird located between the chin and the abdomen.

Brood – The offspring of birds.

Chick – A newly hatched bird; a baby bird.

Cloaca – The aperture through which birds excrete; also the location where eggs and sperm exit the body.

Clutch – The eggs laid by a female bird in a single setting.

Down Feathers – The small feathers that keep a bird warm.

Endemic – Referring to a species that is only found in a particular area.

Fledgling – A young bird that is old enough to leave the nest but still largely depends on the parents.

Flight Feathers – Groups of later feathers found on the wing and tail; includes primary, secondary, and tertiary feathers.

Flock – A group of birds.

Genealogy – The history of the descent of a particular species from its ancestors.

Hatching – The process through which baby birds emerge from the egg.

Hatchling - A newly hatched chick.

Hybrid – The offspring of two different species.

Incubation – The act of resting on eggs to generate heat which causes the eggs to eventually hatch.

Molt – The process through which a bird loses its feathers and grows new ones.

Ornithologist – A professional who studies birds.

Pair Bond – The bond formed between a male and female bird for nesting and breeding purposes.

Pinfeathers – The tiny, developing feathers that emerge from the skin.

Remiges – The wing feathers of a bird.

Retrices – The tail feathers of a bird.

Sexual Dimorphism – Referring to physical differences between the sexes of the same species.

Taxonomy – The classification of species into order, family, genera, etc.

Chapter Two: Understanding Finches

Before you can decide whether or not finches are the right pet for you, you should take the time to learn as much about them as you can. In this chapter you will receive basic information about finches including their taxonomical classification, where they live, what they eat in the wild, their evolutionary history, and different species of finches. Once you have a basic comprehension of what finches are, you will be able to better understand their needs in captivity. You will also be better equipped to decide if they are a good pet for you.

1.) What Are Finches?

Finches are a type of small bird that belong to the order Passeriformes. These birds are largely found in the Northern Hemisphere, but there are a few species found in Neotropic regions. Within the order Passeriformes there are two main families of finches. Birds belonging to the family Fringillidae are often referred to as "true finches" while birds in the family Estrildidae are called waxbills or estrildid finches. Estrildid finches, like the Gouldian finch, are more commonly found in the Old World tropics as well as in Australia.

When it comes to finches, there are a wide variety of different species out there. In fact, half of all bird species belong to the order Passeriformes and there are estimated to be more than 5,000 species within this order. Passerine birds are usually smaller than the birds found in other orders such as Strigiformes (owls) and Galliformes (poultry). Finches and other passerine birds vary from birds belonging to other avian orders in several ways including their anatomy, eggs, nests, and evolutionary history.

Passerine birds, including finches, have four toes on each foot – three toes facing forward and one facing backward – this is referred to as an anisodactyl arrangement. This arrangement of toes enables finches and other passerines to perch not only on horizontal surfaces like branches, but one vertical surfaces like cliffs and tree trunks as well. There is no webbing between the toes as there is with birds belonging to other orders such as Anseriformes (ducks, geese and swans).

Finches also have a special adaptation in their legs which enables them to sleep while they are perched without falling. These birds have a tendon along the back of each leg which causes the muscle to tighten when the leg is bent – when the muscle tightens, the foot curls and becomes stiff. This happens each time the bird lands on a branch and it keeps the bird from falling off a perch even when sleeping.

When it comes to the eggs and nests of passerine birds, chicks emerge from the egg blind and featherless. Finch chicks require a great deal of parental care since the chicks are completely helpless when they emerge from the egg. Passerine birds tend to lay colored eggs while non-passerine birds usually lay white eggs. The clutch size for finches and other passerine birds varies, though the average clutch size is between 2 and 5 eggs, particularly in warmer climates in the Northern Hemisphere.

2.) Facts About Finches

1): Purple Finch (Carpodacus purpureus

As you've already learned, most finches (particularly "true finches") are found in the Northern Hemisphere, though some species can be found in tropical regions as well as in Australia. While the details vary by species, most finches have small bodies with relatively large beaks and flat heads. The smallest species of true finches are the Andean siskin (*Carduelis spinescens*) which stands only 3.8 inches (9.5 cm) tall and the lesser goldfinch (*Carduelis psaltria*) which weighs only about ¼ ounce (8 grams). The largest species of true finch is the collared grosbeak (*Mycerobas affinis*) which stands up to 9.4 inches (24 cm) tall.

For the most part, finches have stubby beaks, the shape of which varies from one species to another. True finches exhibit 12 remiges, or wing feathers, and 9 primary rectrices, or tail feathers. The most common plumage color for finches is brown, often with a green tinge, though many species exhibit a lot of black in their plumage as well. White is largely absent in finches except in bars on the wings. Bright colors like yellow and red are also common, though typically only in males of the species – females often lack the bright coloration exhibited by males. This is referred to as sexual dichromatism.

In terms of habitat, finches are most often found in wooded areas, though some species inhabit mountainous or even desert regions. For example, the house finch is typically found in grasslands or desert while zebra finches tend to inhabit forested areas, typically close to bodies of water. Finches are primarily granivorous – meaning they feed largely on seeds – but some species include a lot of berries and small insects in their diet. Nestlings feed primarily on small arthropods (a type of insect).

The flight pattern of true finches has a bouncing quality to it, alternating between periods of flapping with periods of gliding on closed wings. Most finches sing, with some being very loud and boisterous. The zebra finch, for example, is known to make a variety of different vocalizations and the males of the species have been known to sing very complex songs. Each species exhibits different vocalizations and the song of each bird is unique, though members of the same bloodline often exhibit some similarities in their songs.

Summary of Facts

- **Classification**: most finches belong to the order Passeriformes or Estrildidae
- **Taxonomy**: passerine finches are referred to as "true finches" while finches in the Estrildidae family are called waxbills or estrildid finches
- **Distribution**: most finches are found in the Northern Hemisphere while estrildid finches are found in the Old World tropics and Australia
- **Habitat**: typically found in grasslands or wooded areas, though some species inhabit mountainous or desert regions
- **Anatomical Adaptations**: finches have four toes on each foot (three toes facing forward, one backward); finches have a unique ability to perch on vertical surfaces and they can remain perched while sleeping without falling off
- **Eggs**: passerine finches lay colored eggs with 2 to 5 average per clutch

- **Hatchling**: passerine finches are born blind and featherless; finch chicks require a great deal of parental care
- **Physical Characteristics**: large, often stubby beaks; flat head; short wings
- **Coloration**: brown (often with a green tinge) is common; black is commonly seen on the wings and tail with white plumage largely absent except in wing bars; males often exhibit bright red or yellow coloration
- **Sexual Dimorphism**: females often lack the bright colorings seen on males of many species
- **Diet**: primarily granivorous (eating seeds), though some species eat berries and small arthropods (insects)
- **Vocalization**: most finches sing with some species being very loud and boisterous; each species has a unique vocalization with individual birds having their own song
- **Flight Pattern**: bouncing pattern alternating between periods of flapping with periods of gliding on closed wings
- **Lifespan**: average 4 to 7 years

3.) History of Finches

For many years, the evolutionary history of finches and other passerine birds was largely unknown. Until the late 20th century, families of passerine birds were classified taxonomically into groups based only on their morphological similarities. It was then discovered, however, that these similarities were likely the result of convergent evolution rather than evidence of a genetic relationship. Convergent evolution relates to different species developing similar characteristics that were not necessarily present in the shared ancestor for both species.

An example of convergent evolution that applies to passerine birds is the wren. Different species of wren can be found throughout the Northern Hemisphere as well as in Australia and New Zealand. Many of these species look very similar and exhibit similar behavior patterns, but genetic testing has revealed that these birds are as genetically unrelated as it is possible to be while still remaining part of the order Passeriformes.

Thanks to advances in genetic testing and other aspects of molecular biology, we now know that some of the first passerine birds evolved during the Paleogene or the Late Paleocene era in Gondwana between 55 and 60 million years ago. It is thought that passerine birds evolved from a group of closely-related "near passerines" – a group that contains Piciformes (woodpeckers) and Coraciiformes (kingfishers and todies). Eventually, a radiation of species took place in New Guinea and Australia – from this radiation the songbirds, or Passeri, were born. Later, a large branch of the Passeri clade emerged and expanded into parts of Africa and Eurasia where a number of new lineages were born.

Few fossil remains of true finches have been found, and of those that have been discovered they are largely of species that still exist. It is believed that the true finches evolved sometime during the Middle Miocene, between 10 and 20 million years ago. There is, however, an unidentifiable fossil of some type of finch from the Messinian Age (between 7.3 and 12 million years ago) that was found in Hungary.

Unrelated to true finches are Darwin's finches, or the Galapagos finches. This group of fifteen or so species belongs to the order Passseriformes but they are classified within the family Thraupidae in the subfamily Geospizinae. Though these finches are known to be unrelated to true finches, it is not clear to which bird family they belong. These birds were collected and studied by Charles Darwin during a trip to the Galapagos Islands that was supposed to be concentrated on geology. Throughout his travels, however, Darwin began to recognize similarities in birds found on different islands and even in different countries.

Though Darwin's studies did not originally include finches, he came to use them as a depiction of his theories for the transmutation of species which eventually led to his theory of natural selection. In 1837, Darwin presented his finches along with other bird and mammal specimens to the Geological Society of London. His specimens were then given to John Gould (after whom the Gouldian finch is named) who identified the birds that Darwin originally thought were various species of gross-beaks, finches, and blackbirds as twelve different species belonging to a single group of ground finches.

The term "Darwin's finches" didn't come into use until 1936 when Percy Lowe coined the term – it was then popularized in David Lack's book of the same name which was published in 1947. Further study of Darwin's specimens collected throughout his travels revealed that birds gathered from different islands which were originally thought to be different varieties were actually unique species. This led Darwin to explore further the phenomenon of different finch species being confined to certain islands with each species being uniquely adapted to its environment. Darwin studied the shape and size of the beaks for different species to support his theories.

4.) Types of Finches

There are many different species of finches, though not all of them are kept as pets. Some of the most popular species of finch that are kept as pets include the society finch, the zebra finch, and the Gouldian finch. There are also finches of different colors which are found in the wild throughout the United States which may not be legal to keep as pets including the purple, gold, rose, green, and house finch.

Common Finch Species Kept for Pets:

- Gouldian Finch (*Erythrura gouldiae*)
- Star Finch (*Neochmia ruficauda*)
- Society Finch (*Lonchura striata domestica*)
- Zebra Finch (*Taeniopygia guttata*)

Wild Finches Not Legal for Keeping:

- Purple Finch (*Carpodacus purpureus*)
- House Finch (*Carpodacus mexicanus*)
- American Goldfinch (*Spinus tristis*)
- Common Rosefinch (*Carpodacus erythrinus*)
- European Greenfinch (Chloris chloris)

Gouldian Finch (*Erythrura gouldiae*)

Country of Origin: Australia
Other Names: Lady Gouldian Finch, Rainbow Finch
Size: 5 inches (12.7 cm), 16-17g
Compatibility: passive, can be kept with other passive finch species

The Gouldian Finch is known for its bright coloration. It typically exhibits a green back and purples chest, though there are some white-breasted and yellow-bodied varieties. Other colors that can be found on the Gouldian Finch include bright red, orange, and blue. The female of this species is typically less brightly colored than the male and the blue border around her mask is nearly nonexistent.

In the wild, Gouldian Finches live in groups and they travel by season. During the wet season they inhabit the lowlands where they feast on grass seeds and then they migrate to the surrounding hills during the dry season to breed. Because these birds are from Australia, their breeding season is out of sync with American and European finches. Gouldian Finches typically breed between March and September when day length shortens and temperatures drop between 91° and 66°F.

Gouldian Finches should be fed a diet of high-quality pellets and seed with egg mix as a supplementary source of nutrition. These finches typically lay 4 to 6 eggs per clutch and the eggs hatch about 14 to 16 days after laying. The young hatchlings typically fledge between 20 and 23 days of age and they will be weaned around 6 weeks. Young Gouldians start their first molt between 8 and 10 weeks with a complete molt around 5 to 6 months. It is recommended that you wait until the birds are 6 to 9 months old before breeding them.

Star Finch (*Neochmia ruficauda*)

Country of Origin: Australia
Other Names: Red-Tailed Finch, Red-Faced Finch
Size: 4.25 inches (11cm)
Compatibility: passive, can be kept with other passive finches

The Star Finch is native to northern Australia where it tends to inhabit tall reeds and grasses alongside creeks, rivers and swamps. These birds feed on small insects, millet, and some greens. The Star Finch has a gray-green body with a yellow-green chest and bright red head and face. These birds are named for the star-like white spots on the chest, face and sides. There are some mutations which are yellow-faced or Isabel (lighter, fawn-colored version).

Star Finches are prolific breeders, typically laying clutches of 3 to 6 eggs. These birds breed during the second half of the wet season and their breeding season is fairly lengthy compared to that of other birds. The breeding season typically begins in late December and it has been known to last into March or May. In captivity, Star Finches will breed in mixed company as well as a colony setting and they prefer to build their own nests from raw materials. One thing to keep in mind about this species is that they are "light sitters" – they spook easily so avoid checking the nest until the chicks are 9 or 10 days old.

Society Finch (*Lonchura striata domestica*)

Country of Origin: Asia
Other Names: Bengalese Finch, Bengalee Finch
Size: 4 inches (10 cm)
Compatibility: passive, can be kept with other passive species of finch

The Society Finch is not a species that can be found in the wild. It may have originated as a hybrid of the White-Rumped Munia (or Striated Finch) with finches belonging to the genus *Lonchura*. These birds are highly adapted to life in captivity and they tend to be more accepting of human company and interaction than other finch species. Society finches breed very well in captivity and they can even be used to foster the young of other finch-like species.

Society Finches are not the most colorful birds – they tend to be chocolate brown in color which a scallop of off-white feathers on the chest. There are several color mutations, however, including chocolate pied, white, and fawn pied. It is also important to note that this is a sexually monomorphic species – the males and females are nearly indistinguishable based on their physical characteristics. The best way to tell the sexes apart is through their courtship behavior – the male will sing while the female doesn't tend to.

The Society Finch breeds prolifically in captivity and it is not limited to any particular breeding season. These finches typically have clutches of 3 to 9 eggs which hatch about 16 days after incubation. The birds fledge between day 19 and 25 then they will be weaned at about 4 weeks of age – this is several weeks earlier than some finch species. Society Finches reach sexual maturity at 3 months.

Zebra Finch (*Taeniopygia guttata*)

Country of Origin: Australia
Other Names: Spotted-Sided Finch, Chestnut-Eared Finch
Size: 4 inches (10 cm)
Compatibility: pushy, should be kept with other pushy species

The Zebra Finch is the most common of the estrildid finches and it can be found all over the Australian continent. This species tends to inhabit grasslands and forests, often close to water, and they have been known to take advantage of man-made watering holes. These finches breed any time of year after a substantial rain in their natural habitat. In captivity, they can be bred year-round. Zebra Finches tend to build their nests wherever they can – in scrub brush, trees, on the ground, in rabbit burrows, and more.

Zebra Finches are sexually dimorphic, so males of the species look significantly different than females. Male Zebra Finches exhibit bright orange batches on the check as well as black stripes on the throat. The flanks are chestnut-colored with white spots. Female Zebra Finches have vertical white bars under the eyes, but the rest of their bodies is light grey. Juvenile Zebra Finches look very similar to female adults except t eave a black beak that later turns orange.

The Zebra Finch is a highly adaptable species which makes them a great pet. These finches breed well in captivity, but they require a fairly large enclosure to do so. Zebra Finches can be bred by pair or in colonies, though colonies should consist of no fewer than three pairs to reduce fighting. The average clutch size for Zebra Finches is 4 to 6 eggs and these eggs hatch after 12 to 14 days. These birds fledge between 18 and 22 days then become sexual mature around 3 months. It is recommended, however, that you wait until 6 to 9 months to breed Zebra Finches.

Purple Finch (Carpodacus purpureus)

Country of Origin: Canada, United States
Other Names: none
Size: 5.9 inches (15 cm)
Compatibility: this is a wild finch species

The Purple Finch belongs to the family Fringillidae and it belongs to the same genus as other American Rosefinches. This species can be found throughout Canada and in parts of the northeastern United States – it has also been found along the U.S. Pacific Coast. The Purple Finch tends to inhabit coniferous forested areas where they nest on horizontal branches or in the fork of a tree.

Purple Finches tend to forage for seeds and berries in the trees and brush, though they will also eat some small insects. This species' population declined sharply due to the House Finch. In most cases where these two inches inhabit the same region, the House Finch outcompetes the Purple Finch. The Purple Finch has also seen some competition from the House Sparrow.

The Purple Finch is named for the pink-red color on its head and breast. This color mixes with brown and black moving down toward the belly. Females of the species have no red coloration – instead, they are coarsely streaked and they have strong facial markings.

House Finch (Carpodacus mexicanus)

Country of Origin: North America
Other Names: Hollywood Finch
Size: 5.9 inches (15 cm)
Compatibility: this is a wild finch species

The House Finch is a moderately sized species, growing up to about 5.9 inches (15 cm) and weighing up to 0.95 ounces (27 grams). These finches are found throughout North America, even in Hawaii, and they are widely distributed. For the most part, House Finches are permanent residents, though some of the eastern and northern birds may migrate south during the winter. House Finches were originally native to Mexico, but they were introduced to the United States during the 1940s.

During the 1940s, House Finches were illegally sold as pets in New York under the name Hollywood Finch. To avoid being punished under the rules of the Migratory Bird Treaty Act, owners and vendors released the birds into the wild. Since then, the House Finch has become naturalized and it has been known to displace and outcompete native species like the Purple Finch and the House Sparrow. There is an estimated population of up to 1.7 billion House Sparrows across the North American continent.

American Goldfinch (Spinus tristis)

Country of Origin: North America
Other Names: Eastern Goldfinch
Size: 5.5 inches (14 cm)
Compatibility: this is a wild finch species

The American Goldfinch is a fairly small species that lives in North America but migrates from parts of Canada and the northern U.S. as far south as Mexico during the winter. This species is known for its vibrant yellow coloration, though this color is only seen during the breeding season. During non-breeding season, males of the species exhibit an olive coloration and the female is a dull brownish shade of yellow – she brightens a little in the summer.

The American Goldfinch thrives in open country like meadows, fields, and flood plains, though they can also be found in orchards and gardens. These birds are diurnal feeders which means that they are largely active during the day. American Goldfinches are primarily granivorous, though they will sometimes eat insects and may feed them to their young for protein. What makes these finches unique is that they use their feet extensively for feeding, often hanging from seed heads to better reach the seeds.

Common Rosefinch (Carpodacus erythrinus)

Country of Origin: Europe and Asia
Other Names: Scarlet Rosefinch, Scarlet Grosbeak
Size: 5.9 inches (15 cm)
Compatibility: this is a wild finch species

The Common Rosefinch is the most widely distributed species of Rosefinch found in Europe and Asia. This species is a little larger than a sparrow and it has a conical-shaped bill. Males of the species exhibit a bright rose-colored head, rump, and breast with dark brown wings and a white belly. The female of the species (as well as juvenile males) is more dull-colored with a yellowish-brown body with slightly brighter coloration on the rump and head with a buff-colored chest.

The Common Rosefinch has been working its way across Europe, breeding everywhere from England to Afghanistan. These birds tend to inhabit woodlands or thickets during the summer and, during the winter, they move to gardens and orchards where they can still find food. This species tends to build its nests in low bushes, laying clutches of up to 5 dark blue eggs with brown spots.

European Greenfinch (Chloris chloris)

Country of Origin: Europe
Other Names: Greenfinch
Size: 5.9 inches (15 cm)
Compatibility: this is a wild finch species

The European Greenfinch is widely distributed throughout Europe and into parts of southwest Asia and northern Africa. This species is typically a permanent resident, though some northern populations migrate south during the winter. In addition to being widely distributed throughout Europe, this finch species has also been introduced into Australia and New Zealand. In Malta, the species has been frequently trapped, domesticated, and bred for its singing abilities.

The European Greenfinch is similar to the house sparrow in size and shape but it has a green overall coloration with yellow on the tail and wings. Females and juveniles of the species are duller in coloration with more brown tones on the back. These birds have a thick, conical beak and their song contains a mix of trilling twitters and wheezes. The flight pattern of this species is "butterfly-like".

The European Greenfinch tends to inhabit woodland areas as well as farmland hedges and gardens where the vegetation is fairly thick. These birds nest in bushes or trees, laying clutches of 3 to 6 eggs. Outside the breeding season, these finches tend to form very large flocks, often mixing with other finches and buntings. The breeding season lasts from mid-March through June with hatchlings beginning to fledge in early July.

Chapter Three: What to Know Before You Buy

2: Star Finch (Neochmia ruficauda)

Now that you know the basics about finches including where they come from and the most popular species, you can begin to think about the practical aspects of keeping finches in captivity. Not only do you need to determine whether you need a license for keeping finches in your area, but you should also think about whether you can keep finches with other pets, how many you should keep together, and how much it costs to keep finches. You will learn all of this information and more in this chapter.

1.) Do You Need a License?

Before you attempt to keep finches as pets, you need to make sure that it is legal for you to do so. Laws vary from one country to another, and even from one region to another within the same country, in regard to the keeping of certain species of animal as pets. You would be wise to check with your local council to make sure you do not need a license to keep finches as pets in your area.

a.) Licensing in the U.S.

When it comes to legally keeping finches in the United States, you need to be very careful. It is only legal to keep birds that have been bred and raised in captivity – any species that is found in the wild is not legal to keep as a pet. In 1918, the United States passed the Migratory Bird Treaty Act to protect native species. This act makes it "illegal for anyone to take, possess, import, export, transport, sell, purchase, barter, or offer for sale, purchase, or barter, any migratory bird, or the parts, nests, or eggs of such a bird except under the terms of a valid permit issued pursuant to Federal regulations."

Under this act, it is illegal to keep finches that are native to the United States – this includes the following species:
- Eurasian Bullfinch (*Pyrrhula pyrrhula*)

- Common Chaffinch (*Fringilla coelebs*)
- Cassin's Finch (*Carpodacus cassinii*)
- American Goldfinch (*Spinus tristis*)
- Oriental Greenfinch (*Chloris sinica*)
- Hawfinch (*Coccathraustes coccathraustes*)
- Common Rosefinch (*Carpodacus erythrinus*)
- Black Rosy-Finch (*Leucosticte atrata*)
- Puerto Rican Bullfinch (*Loxigilla portoricensis*)
- Gray-Crowned Rosy-Finch (*Leucosticte tephrocotis*)
- Purple Finch (*Carpodacus purpureus*)
- House Finch (*Carpodacus mexicanus*)
- Lesser Goldfinch (*Spinus psaltria*)
- Laysan Finch (*Telespiza ultima*)
- Nihoa Finch (*Telespiza ultima*)

The only way you will be able to legally keep one of the species on this list is to obtain a license from the U.S. Fish and Wildlife Service. These permits are only issued to qualified applicants for scientific purposes, rehabilitation or educational purposes, or taxidermy. For more information about receiving a permit, speak to your Regional Bird Permit Office.

Though you may not need a license or a permit to keep captive-bred species of finches like the Zebra Finch, the Society Finch and the Gouldian Finch, you will need a permit if you intend to breed your finches. These permits are typically issued by the state and regulations will vary from one state to another. To apply for a bird breeder license you will need to contact your local council to submit an application and to pay the associated fee.

b.) Licensing in the U.K. and Australia

Licensing requirements for pets in the UK are much less strict than they are in the United States. It is just as illegal in the UK to keep dangerous or endangered animals in the U.S., but there are fewer regulations for pets. One thing you do need to be aware of in terms of licensing for finches in the UK is related to importing, exporting, or traveling with your pet. In the UK you must obtain an animal movement license in order to travel with your pet into or out of the country. If you purchase your finches from someone outside the UK, you must also obtain a pet bird import license and the bird must be properly identified and it will have to go through a 30-day quarantine prior to movement to prevent the spread of disease.

In both the UK and Australia, you do not need a license or permit to keep non-native species as pets. This includes the following finch species:
- Blue-faced parrot finch (*Erythrura trichroa*)
- Gouldian finch (*Erythrura gouldiae*)

- Painted finch (*Emblema pictum*)
- Star finch (*Neochmia ruficauda*)
- Society finch (*Lonchura striata domestica*)
- Zebra finch (*Taeniopygia guttata*)

Before you purchase finches in the UK or Australia, just make sure that the breeder or supplier obtained the birds legally or, if they were bred on-site, that they have the proper breeding license. Again, if you purchase your finches from someone outside the country, you will need to obtain an animal movement license and go through the proper procedure to have your birds imported.

2.) How Many Should You Buy?

Finches may be small but they are very active birds. These birds are naturally very social so they need to be kept in groups or pairs. Depending on the number of finches you decide to keep, you may need to adjust the size of the cage to give all of your finches adequate flying space. Finches cannot be tamed like other pet birds and they do not enjoy a great deal of human interaction. For this reason it is very important that you provide for the social needs of your finches by keeping them in pairs or groups.

3.) Can Finches Be Kept with Other Pets?

While finches are very social and they like to be kept with others of their own kind, they do not necessarily get along well with other birds, even other finches. If you want to keep multiple species together, make sure that they are of similar size and disposition. For example, you should not house two aggressive species like the melba finch with other similar species, especially those with red masks like the star finch. Remember, as is true with any pet, individual finches will have their own personalities so even if two finches are calm and passive on their own, they will not necessarily get along with other finches.

Below you will find a list of passive finch species that typically get along well with others:

- Red and green Avadavats
- Black-cheeked waxbill
- Black-rumped waxbill
- Blue-breasted parrot finch
- Blue-faced parrot finch
- Bronze-winged mannikan
- Chestnut-breasted finch
- Common waxbill
- Gold breasted waxbill
- Green twinspots (except with star finch)
- Gouldian finch

- Masked grass finch
- Owl finch
- Painted finch
- Pin-tailed parrot finch
- Red-headed parrot finch
- Society finch
- Spice finch
- Star finch
- Yellow-rumped finch

The following finch species can be a little pushy – they can be housed with other finches as long as the enclosure is very large and there are decorations/accessories in place to break up sightlines:

- Aurora finch
- Dark fire finch
- European goldfinch
- Green singing finch
- Lavender finch
- Purple grenadier
- Shaft-tail finch
- Zebra finch

In addition to the species listed, you may also be able to house your finches with canaries as long as they are similar in size and temperament. Never house finches with parrots.

4.) *Ease and Cost of Care*

Before you decide to go out and buy a couple of finches, you need to make sure that you are able to provide for all of your finches' needs. Not only do you need to buy the finches, but you also have to cover the cost of a cage and cage accessories, plus food and basic medical care. In this section you will find an overview of the costs associated with keeping finches divided into two categories – initial costs and monthly costs – as well as average estimates for each cost.

a.) Initial Costs

The initial costs for keeping finches as pets include those costs you must cover before you can bring your finches home – it also includes the cost of the birds themselves. Some of the initial costs you will need to cover include the cage, cage accessories, perches/toys, a nest, and supplies for nail/wing clipping. You will find an overview of each of these costs as well as an estimate for each cost below:

Purchase Price – The purchase price for finches will vary from one species to another but, for the most part, you can expect to spend about $15 to $25 per bird (£9.75 - £16.25).

Cage – Because finches are small birds, they do not require as large a cage as a parrot or macaw – the cage also doesn't need to be built with heavy-duty materials. The cost of your finch cage will vary by size and materials – it also depends how many finches you intend to keep. On average, you should expect to spend between $40 and $150 (£26 - £97.50) on a medium- to large-sized cage for a group of finches.

Cage Accessories – In addition to your finch cage, you also need to provide certain accessories including a food dish, a water dish, a nest, and a bird bath. For these expenses you should expect to spend between $25 and $50 (£16.25 - £32.50).

Perches/Toys – Birds are very intelligent creatures, so they require an assortment of toys, perches, and ladders in their cage to keep them mentally engaged. For finches you do not need to purchase very large or heavy-duty toys but you should provide at least four different toys, several perches, a ladder, and a play stand. To cover these costs you can expect to spend between $100 and $200 (£65 - £130).

Nail/Wing Clipping – Part of caring for pet birds will involve clipping their nails and trimming their wings. Though you will need to perform these tasks on a regular basis, you will only need to purchase the supplies (nail clippers and wing scissors) once. The average cost for nail/wing clipping supplies is between $15 and $25 (£9.75 - £16.25).

Initial Costs for Keeping Finches	
Expense	**Average Cost**
Purchase Price	$15 to $25 per bird (£9.75 - £16.25 each)
Cage	$40 to $150 (£26 - £97.50)
Cage Accessories	$25 to $50 (£16.25 - £32.50)
Perches/Toys	$100 to $200 (£65 - £130)
Nail/Wing Clipping	$15 to $25 (£9.75 - £16.25)
Total:	$195 to $450 (£127 - £293)

b.) Monthly Costs

The monthly costs for keeping finches as pets include those costs which recur on a monthly basis. The most important monthly cost is food but you also need to think about things like cage liners, cleaning supplies and veterinary exams. You will find an overview of each of these costs as well as an estimate for each cost below:

Bird Food – Finches are fairly small so they do not eat a great deal of food at any given time. If you keep a group of finches, however, your food costs will be higher than if you only kept a pair of finches. Finches require a high-quality diet of finch seed mix supplemented with sprouted seeds, fresh greens, egg, and a calcium supplement like a cuttlebone. You should budget for about 2 teaspoons of seed per bird per day plus fresh greens and other supplementary foods. The average monthly cost to feed a pair of finches is about $20 (£13) with a larger group of finches requiring a budget up to $50 (£32.50) per month for the cost of food.

Cage Liners – Most bird cages come with a removable tray in the bottom which makes it easy to clean the cage. To make cleanup even easier, you can line this tray with a cage liner or even something as simple as newspaper. If you use newspaper you may not have to pay anything but, if you buy special cage liners, you may purchase a roll of flexible lining for about $15 to $25 (£9.75 - £16.25) which will last you at least a month.

Cleaning Supplies – In addition to changing the liner for your finch cage on a regular basis, you also need to clean the cage and your cage accessories. The cost for cleaning supplies is fairly low and you will not need to buy them every month. For the sake of budgeting, however, you should plan for about $5 (£3.25) per month in cleaning supplies.

Veterinary Exam – In order to keep your finches in good health, you should have them examined by a veterinarian once a year. You will not be able to take your birds to just any vet because not all of them are qualified to treat birds. An avian veterinary exam can cost anywhere from $50 to $200 (£32.50 - £130) including the cost of vaccinations. The more birds you have, the higher your costs will be. For a pair of finches, you can expect to spend between $100 and $400 (£65 - £260) per year which, averaged over 12 months, equates to a monthly cost of about $8 to $33 (£5.20 - £21.50).

Monthly Costs for Keeping Finches	
Expense	**Average Cost**
Bird Food	$20 to $50 (£13 - £32.50)
Cage Liners	$15 to $25 (£9.75 - £16.25)
Cleaning Supplies	$5 (£3.25)
Veterinary Exam	$8 to $33 (£5.20 - £21.50)
Total:	$48 to $113 (£31 - £74)

5.) Pros and Cons of Finches

Finches are beautiful birds that can make wonderful pets, but they are not the right choice for everyone. Before you decide to keep finches as pets, you should consider both the pros and cons. Below you will find a list of the pros and cons associated with finches as pets to help you make an informed decision:

Pros for Finches as Pets

- Finches are very attractive birds – they come in a wide variety of colors and patterns.

- Because of their small size, finches are much more manageable and practical to keep than parrots and other large birds.
- Finches generally do not bite like some birds do, though they don't enjoy human interaction as much as parrots.
- Compared to other birds, finches are a fairly low-maintenance option.
- Finches are much less expensive than other birds to purchase and to maintain.

Cons for Finches as Pets

- Though they are not as loud as parrots and macaws, finches can be rather noisy – especially zebra finches.
- Finches generally do not enjoy human interaction the way parrots do, but some of them can be hand-tamed.
- Some species can be very territorial, especially during breeding, so you may need a very large cage if you intend to keep several finches, especially of different species.
- Finches can be a little messy, flinging seed across the room at times.

Chapter Four: Purchasing Finches

After reviewing some of the practical aspects of keeping finches in the last chapter, you may be ready to think about actually purchasing some finches. In this chapter you will receive tips for where to find different species of finches as well as some information about picking out healthy birds. When shopping around for finches it is essential that you choose a reputable breeder or supplier so the birds you bring home are healthy. This will save you the hassle and expense of repeated visits to the vet and it will ensure that your finches lead longer, happier lives.

1.) Where to Buy Finches

If you have decided that finches truly are the right pet for you, you need to start thinking about where you are going to get them. Below you will find recommendations for where to find finches in both the U.S. and the UK.

a.) Buying in the U.S.

In the United States, finding finches for sale may be as easy as going to your local pet store. Many of the larger pet stores carry both zebra finches and society finches – you may even be able to find rare colorations or other species at some stores. If you do not have a particular color or species in mind, going to a pet store might be the right option for you. If, however, you know that you want a certain color or a particular species, your best bet may be to go directly to a breeder for your finches.

Below you will find links to several finch breeders in the United States:

The Finch Farm.
<http://www.thefinchfarm.com/finchesforsale>

The White Finch Aviary.
<https://lebeaupinson.wordpress.com/>

Breeders – The Finch Information Center.
<http://www.finchinfo.com/resources/links/finch_breeders.
php>

BirdBreeders.com.
<http://www.birdbreeders.com/birds/category/finches>

Fabulous Finch. <http://www.fabulousfinch.com/>

Acadiana Aviaries. < http://www.zebrafinch.com/>

b.) Buying in the U.K.

Purchasing finches in the UK is very similar to purchasing
them in the United States. Many pet stores carry finches as
part of their regular stock, though the species and color
varieties may vary from one store to another. If you have a
certain color or species in mind, you may want to look
around for a local breeder. To find a local breeder you can
ask around at pet stores, do an online search, or ask your
local veterinarian for recommendations.

Below you will find links to several finch breeders in the
United Kingdom:

Riverside Aviaries.
<http://www.riversideaviaries.co.uk/birds.htm>

Telford Bird Breeders.
<http://telfordbirdbreeders.co.uk/Bengalese-Finch.html>

"The Australian Finch Society."
<http://www.australianfinchsociety.co.uk/salesandwants.ht
m>

The Waxbill Finch Society.
<http://www.waxbillfinchsociety.org.uk/wfs_fs.html>

BirdTrader.co.uk.
<http://www.birdtrader.co.uk/Finches/A/passerine-for-
sale.php#KywC00sBSdqtMo4G.97>

2.) How to Select a Healthy Finches

When it comes time to purchase your finches, you should take the time to not only select a reputable breeder but to choose a healthy bird as well. If you purchase your finches from the pet store, you may not be seeing them in their ideal state. The pet store can be a stressful environment for a bird, especially if the birds are kept in small, cramped cages with little space for them to fly. <u>If you choose to buy your finches from a breeder, follow the steps below to choose a trustworthy breeder</u>:

1. Perform some basic research to find several different breeders in your area – you can ask at various pet

stores for the names of breeders, perform a web search, or ask your veterinarian for references.

2. Compile a list of breeder information and visit each of their websites to see what you can learn about them – if they do not have a website you will need to just call and talk to them.

3. In reviewing the website for each breeder, determine whether the breeder seems to be knowledgeable and experienced with finches.

4. Call each breeder and ask a few questions to determine the breeder's experience and knowledge with finches – if the breeder cannot answer your questions satisfactorily, or if he refuses to answer questions, you should move on to the next option.

5. Ask each breeder about his breeding policies – What kind of conditions are the birds kept in? How often are they bred? Does the breeder keep records of each breeding?

6. Narrow down your list of breeders to only those that seem experienced and knowledgeable – you do not want to buy from a breeder who doesn't take good care of his birds.

7. Visit the remaining breeders on your list to see some of the birds they have available for sale.

8. Evaluate the conditions in which the birds are kept and observe the birds themselves for signs of good health.

9. If the birds are kept in small, cramped cages or if they do not appear to be in good health, move on to the next breeder – you may be tempted to "rescue" a bird from an irresponsible breeder but this may only result in you having to pay expensive medical bills down the line.

10. Choose the breeder that you feel has the healthiest birds and the one that has the type of finch in the color you want.

11. If the birds are not yet old enough to take home, you may need to put down a deposit or pay for them upfront to reserve them for when they are old enough to take home.

In addition to evaluating the breeder's knowledge and expertise, you should also observe the birds themselves to make sure they are in good condition. Before you bring home any finches, you should ensure that they are healthy. Follow the tips below to determine whether a finch is in good health or not:

- The cages in which the birds are kept should be clean and in good repair – if the cage is dirty or cramped, there is a good chance that the birds are sick or stressed.

- A healthy finch will be active and alert – if the birds appear sluggish or if they are hiding in the corner rather than moving around the cage, they may be sick.

- Check the birds' eyes – they should be clear and bright with no discharge or clouding. Runny eyes or squinting can be indicative of infection.

- Evaluate the bird's plumage – the feathers should be clean and bright rather than dull or scruffy.

- Check the bird's beak for signs of infection – if the bird has an infection it will likely exhibit discharge or crust on the nares (nostrils).

- Observe the birds at feeding time, if possible, to make sure that they have a healthy appetite – if the birds aren't eating, it could be a sign of illness.

- Interact with the birds, if possible, to gauge their temperament. Finches are not especially fond of human interaction but they may be curious about humans and they should not be overly aggressive toward them.

- Make sure that the finches are fully weaned and that they have developed their adult feathers before bringing them home.

If, after observing and interacting with the finches, you are able to determine that they seem healthy you can think about actually purchasing them and taking them home. Again, while it may be tempting to "rescue" a bird from poor conditions there is a greater likelihood of the bird dying from a disease it has already contracted or of it succumbing to stress.

Chapter Five: Caring for Finches

Before you actually go out and buy your finches, you should take some time to review their needs for habitat and diet. In this chapter you will receive detailed information about keeping finches in captivity including how to build and decorate their habitat as well as tips for providing your finches with a healthy diet. You will also receive information about training and taming your finches. Before buying any finches, make sure that you can provide for them everything they need.

1.) Habitat Requirements

Finches are cage birds which simply means that, unlike other pet birds like parrots, they will spend their entire lives in a cage. For this reason, it is essential that you provide your finches with a cage that gives them enough space to fly for exercise. Finches are naturally very active and social birds, so they need to be kept in groups – this means that you'll also have to provide a large enough cage to accommodate several finches. In this section you will receive specific tips for choosing the right cage for your finches and for decorating it appropriately.

a.) Minimum Cage Requirements

Different finch species will grow to different sizes but, for the most part, finches grow between 3 and 8 inches (7.6 to 20.3 cm) in length. To ensure that your finches have enough space to fly, it is recommended that you provide at least 3 to 4 square feet (0.9 to 1.2 square meters) of floor space per finch. The minimum recommended cage height for finches is 16 inches (40.6 cm) and your finch cage should be longer than it is tall. It is never recommended that you house finches in a round cage because this will disrupt their natural flight pattern.

Below you will find a chart detailing the minimum cage requirements for different numbers of finches. Remember, finches are social birds and should be kept, at a minimum, in pairs.

# of Finches	Cage Length	Cage Width
2	18 in (45.7 cm)	24 in (61 cm)
3 to 4	24 in (60.9 cm)	36 in (91.4 cm)
4 to 6	30 in (76.2 cm)	46 in (116.8cm)
6 to 8	36 in (91.4 cm)	52 in (132 cm)
8 to 10	42 in (106.6 cm)	60 in (152.4 cm)
10 to 14	48 in (121.9 cm)	64 in (162.5 cm)

Again, the minimum cage height recommended for finches in 16 inches (40.6 cm), though it should be higher in larger cages with more finches. Cage height is not as important as cage length, however. No matter how high your cage is, your finches will likely congregate at the top because they feel more secure when they are up high. For this reason you need to make sure the cage is long enough to accommodate several perches and nests in the upper regions of the cage so each finch has its own personal space.

b.) Cage Accessories and Toys

The most important accessories and toys you need to have
in your finch cage include the following:

- Food and water dishes
- Perches
- Toys
- Nest/nesting materials

For your finches' food and water bowls, you should choose
a material that is easy to clean and disinfect – stainless steel
is the best option. A good second option would be plastic or
glass dishes – do not use metal dishes that have been
soldered at the seams because this could lead to lead
poisoning. Position your food and water bowls at opposite
ends of the cage and, if you have more than two finches in
your cage, consider adding extra food and water dishes.

Perches are very important for your finch cage and you
should provide several different types. The best perches for
finch cages are made from clean hardwood branches –
never use anything that has been sprayed with pesticide
and avoid using branches that are molding or rotted. Make
sure when you place the perches in your cage that you do
not position them directly above each other – space them
out so they do not become contaminated with bird
droppings. You will need to replace your perches every so

often because you cannot disinfect wood and they will eventually become covered in droppings.

For toys, you should provide an assortment of different options because your finches will appreciate variety. One good option to include is a swing – make sure you position it so it can move freely without hitting the wall of the cage. Some finches also enjoy ropes and ladders – just avoid using toys made from yarn or small synthetic fibers that your finches could consume and choke on. If you have a very large cage for your finches you can even include some large silk plants or nontoxic live plants as decoration.

Another important element to include in your finch cage is nests and nesting materials. Finches can be prolific breeders, even in captivity, so you need to provide them with adequate nesting space. Some finches will accept artificial nest boxes while others prefer baskets or loose nesting material to build their own nests. To provide your finches with a place to roost at night, position at least one nest box in the upper corner of the cage. If you choose a wooden nesting box, keep in mind that you'll have to replace it eventually as it becomes contaminated with droppings. Plastic and metal nest boxes can be cleaned and disinfected, but they may also be prone to temperature fluctuations which may not be good for your finches.

c.) Building Your Own Finch Cage

If you cannot find a cage that will meet the needs of your finches, or if you simply want to customize your finch cage, you may want to think about building your own cage. You can purchase metal cage segments from various online suppliers to build a custom cage, or you can use unconventional materials like an old wardrobe. Another option is to construct a wooden frame and then enclose it with metal wire to contain your finches.

When building a homemade finch cage, be very careful to use only non-toxic materials. Avoid using redwood, cedar, pressure-treated wood, and screen as well as certain metals like copper, zinc, lead, or brass. If you use galvanized wire to enclose your finch cage, make sure to wash it well with vinegar and a hardwire brush before using it – this will help to prevent zinc and lead poisoning. The best building materials to use include: industrial-grade epoxy paint, exterior-grade plywood, PVC powder-coated galvanized wire, and all-plastic hardware netting.

d.) Lighting and Temperature

In addition to providing your finches with an appropriate cage, you also have to monitor the lighting and temperature to which they are exposed. The best lighting for a finch cage is natural, direct sunlight or a light from a full-spectrum bulb which mimics natural sunlight. The only way to utilize direct natural light is with an outdoor enclosure – indoor enclosures will require supplemental lighting. Not only does full-spectrum lighting mimic natural sunlight, but it also provides ultra-violet (UV) light which helps your finches to manufacture vitamin D3 – this vitamin is essential for building healthy bones.

When using artificial lighting for your finch cage, you should try to mimic a natural light cycle. This can help to facilitate more natural reproductive patterns and it will also impact your finch's molt. Your best bet is to plug your lights in to an automatic timer that will turn them on at sunrise and off at sunset. You may need to adjust the timing for your lights every few weeks as seasonal changes affect natural day length.

In terms of temperature, finches can survive in a wide range of temperatures as low as near-freezing and as high as 90°F (32°C). The ideal temperature for finches, however, is between 70°F and 80°F (21° to 27°C). If you keep your finches outdoors, bring them inside when the temperature drops below 68°F (20°C) or provide them with a heat source. Like many animals, finches can succumb to heat stroke so it is important that if temperatures reach 90°F (32°C) that you provide them with a way to cool off.

Finches can not only adjust to a wide range of temperatures, but they can adjust to different humidity levels as well. The recommended humidity level for finches will vary from one species to another depending where the finch's natural habitat lies. For finches from subtropical areas (and for breeding finches), a humidity level between 50% and 70% is recommended. You can alter the humidity in your finch cage easily by providing a bird bath or by misting the cage occasionally with clean water.

2.) Feeding Finches

In the wild, finches feed primarily on seed though some species eat berries and small arthropods (insects) as well. To ensure that your finches stay happy and healthy in captivity, you need to provide them with a high-quality diet. You should not feed your finches just one type of seed and seeds alone are not enough – you need to offer your finches a variety of seeds and a supplemental diet that includes fresh greens, eggs, and a source of calcium like a cuttlebone. In this section you will receive detailed information for creating a healthy diet for your finches.

a.) Nutritional Needs of Finches

Finches require unlimited access to fresh water in addition to a healthy, varied diet. You can buy seed mixes at your local pet store which contain several different types of seed or you can create your own mix yourself. Seed-only diets can lead to severe nutritional deficiencies in finches, especially for juvenile birds. This does not mean, however, that you cannot use a commercial bird feed for your finches – it just means that you have to provide supplementary sources of nutrition to balance everything out.

Just like any living thing, finches require a balance of protein, carbohydrate and fat in their diet – they also require certain vitamins and minerals. <u>You will find an overview of the nutritional needs for finches below</u>:

- **Protein** – Protein is constructed from amino acids and they are essential for the production of healthy bone, feather, muscle and hormones in finches – it can also be a source of energy. Different species of finches have different needs for protein, but all finches need 10 essential amino acids in their diet which their bodies cannot produce. These amino acids include valine, leucine, isoleucine, lysine, histidine, arginine, tryptophan, threonine, methionine, and phenylalanine. Finches receive some of their protein needs from seeds but you should also supplement their diet with egg or live insects to ensure that their needs for protein are met. Egg is the best source of complete protein for finches.

- **Carbohydrate** – For finches, carbohydrates are the main source of energy and it is the only energy source that can be utilized by the nervous system. Deficiencies in carbohydrate can result in neurological problems as well as hypoglycemia.

- **Fat** – Birds require certain essential fatty acids to support the production of cells and membranes – some types of fat are also used for energy. The most important fatty acid for finches is linoleic acid. While fats are an important part of the diet for finches, a diet too high in fat can lead to health problems such as the malabsorption of nutrients – diets too low in fat, on the other hand, can lead to weight loss and immune system deficiencies.

- **Vitamins** – Finches require a variety of different vitamins in their diet and these vitamins can be divided into two categories: fat-soluble and water-soluble. Fat-soluble vitamins can be stored in the body for longer periods of time than water-soluble vitamins. The most important fat-soluble vitamins for finches include vitamin D3, vitamin E, vitamin A, and vitamin K. Water-soluble vitamins that are necessary for finches include riboflavin, niacin, thiamin, biotin, pantothenic acid, vitamin B12, vitamin C, pyridoxine, and choline.

- **Minerals** – Various minerals are essential for finches because they help to support bone growth, muscle function and egg production. The most important minerals for finches include phosphorus, calcium, magnesium, copper, iron, selenium, zinc, iodine, sodium, manganese, and chlorine. Calcium is the most important mineral for finches.

b.) Types of Food

Your best bet for providing for the nutritional needs of your finches is to offer them a commercial feed that is specially formulated for finches. This feed should account for about 70% of your finches' diet while supplementary foods account for the rest. Finches have been known to enjoy various fresh foods including kale, lettuce, spinach, dandelion greens, carrot tops and even some fruits like apples and pears. Sprouted seeds and spray millet are also excellent supplementary food choices for finches.

To make your own seed mix for finches you can combine several different types of seeds – it is recommended that you use at least three different types. <u>Some recommended seeds to include in your mix are</u>:

- Canary grass seed
- White millet
- Plate millet
- Panicum millet
- Japanese millet
- Niger seed

Different species of finches have different preferences for certain types of seed. You should try out several different types with your finches to find out what they like best and then include these seeds in your mix. If you make your own seed mix you should include 3 parts of seed mix and 1 part soft food. A soft food may include some type of egg mix or nesting mix.

c.) Feeding Tips and Amount to Feed

Finches in the wild do not actually eat their seeds whole – they hull them first - so they do not require grit in their diet like some birds do. Providing your finches with a cuttlebone or some other source of calcium will help to keep their beak strong enough to hull seeds efficiently. The lime found in cuttlebone also helps to ensure healthy digestion for finches.

When offering your finches supplementary foods like fruits or vegetables, it is best to offer them in small, bite-sized amounts. The ideal size for supplementary foods is no larger than a very small blueberry. Offer your supplementary foods sparingly, favoring fresh greens over fruits for the valuable minerals they can provide. You should also make sure to vary the rotation of your supplementary foods so your finches do not become bored with their diet.

When it comes to seed, most finches will consume between 1 and 2 teaspoons of seed per day. Finches do not tend to overeat, though you may notice them eating a little bit more than usual during the winter and when they are molting. Be careful about buying too much seed at once because you do not want it to go bad before you can use it. At the very most, you should buy enough seed to last you a month. Some finch owners also recommend freezing commercial seed mixes for seven days before feeding it to your finches to kill any moth or beetle larvae that may have gotten into the mix.

3.) Handling and Taming Finches

Finches are very different from parrots and other pet birds in that they do not tend to enjoy human interaction. It is possible to tame finches to some degree, but you are unlikely to have any success in training them and they may never actually like being handled. Even though you should not handle your finches on a regular basis, there may come a time when you need to catch your finch – either to trim his nails and wings, or to take him to the veterinarian. <u>The proper procedure for catching a finch is listed below</u>:

1. Purchase a finch net – these are available in different sizes but they typically consist of very fine mesh attached to a plastic or wood frame with a long handle.

2. Wait for the finch to land on the floor or the wall of the cage where there is enough space around him to put the net down.

3. Maneuver the opening of the net over the finch, covering him completely.

4. Gently tap the net on the side of the cage to scare the bird further into the net.

5. Carefully turn the net so it droops over the frame, holding your bird inside, and retrieve the net from the cage.

6. After removing the net from the cage, place your hand under the bird and carefully cup it to keep the finch from escaping.

If you do not have a finch net or if you prefer not to use one, you can also catch your finch by hand by following the steps listed below:

1. Remove all of the perches from the cage before you attempt to catch your finch.

2. Wait for the finch to land on the floor or on the side of the cage.

3. Quickly but carefully pin the finch to the floor or the wall by cupping your hand around him.

4. Gently close your fist around the bird, securing his wings to the side of his body so he cannot escape, then remove your hand from the cage with the finch in tow.

a.) Trimming Your Finch's Nails

Some species of finch will need their nails trimmed more often than others for their own safety. If your finch's nails grow too long and sharp, they could get caught on toys or other accessories in the cage and it could result in broken toes. Certain species like zebra finches may require rare trimming while society finches and owl finches require occasional trimming. Species that need frequent nail trimming include strawberry finches, waxbills, and orange cheeks.

To trim your finch's nails, you will need to purchase a set of bird nail trimmers and a vial of styptic powder. Once you have caught your finch, maneuver it in your hand by making a loose fist around its body with your thumb and forefinger around the neck so it can't wriggle free. You can then use your thumb and middle finger to hold the bird's foot while you trim its nails. Separate the toes and make a quick, clean cut through the tip of the nail. Keep in mind that the nail contains a blood vessel, called the quick, and if you sever it the toe will bleed – this is when you will need to use the styptic powder to stop the bleeding.

Because finches use their longest two toes – their back toe and front toe – to perch, you should leave these two nails a little bit longer. The middle two toe nails can be cut fairly short. It is recommended that you have your veterinarian show you how to properly clip your finch's nails before you try it yourself so you don't hurt your bird.

b.) Clipping a Finch's Wings

The reason bird owners clip their birds' wings is to limit their flight. Not only does this help to keep the bird from escaping, but it also keeps the bird from flying away when the owner is handling it – this helps with hand-taming the bird. Cage birds like finches cannot be tamed in the way that parrots can and they need to be able to fly in order to get enough exercise to be healthy in captivity. This being the case, it is not recommended that you clip your finch's wings at all.

Chapter Six: Breeding Finches

One of the things people love about finches as pets is that they can be very prolific breeders. In many cases, you do not need to do anything more than put a male and a female in the same cage with some nesting material to encourage the two to breed. Breeding finches can be a wonderful experience but it is not a decision you should make lightly. In this chapter you will receive valuable information about the breeding process for finches as well as some tips for hatching and raising baby finches.

1.) Basic Breeding Info

Breeding your finches can be an exciting experience, but there are some challenges you may need to overcome. Before you set out to breed your birds, take the time to learn about cultivating a healthy breeding pair as well as the basics about finch breeding behavior. The first step in breeding your finches is to select a breeding pair which begins with being able to tell the two sexes apart.

a.) Differentiating Between the Sexes

Some species of finches are sexually dimorphic which simply means that there are physical differences between the two sexes that can be assessed visually. In these cases, the male of the species is typically more brightly colored or he may exhibit more elaborate markings than the female. Some examples of finch species which exhibit sexual dimorphism include the Gouldian finch and the cordon bleu waxbill. In both of these species the male is more brightly and extensively colored while the female exhibits paler versions of the male colors.

Even with sexually dimorphic species of finch it can be difficult to tell between the sexes for certain color varieties or mutations. For example, the white zebra finch is all-white in color so neither sex exhibits any distinguishing markings. You also need to consider the fact that some finch species exhibit seasonal changes in their plumage. The males and females of certain species like the strawberry finch look almost identical in non-breeding season but the male might develop color changes or pattern changes during breeding season. In cases like this, the coloring of the male might become brighter or more vibrant during breeding season.

To add to the difficulty of sexing finches, you also need to consider the fact that some species are not sexually dimorphic at all – these species are referred to with the term sexually monomorphic. These finches do not exhibit any visual differences between the two sexes, even during breeding season. An example of a sexually monomorphic finch species is the society finch. In the case of sexually monomorphic species, non-visual characteristics must be evaluated to tell the sexes apart. In some species, only the male, the cock, will sing – even in species where both sexes sing, the song of the hen may be shorter or less elaborate. The most obvious way to tell the sexes of sexually monomorphic species apart is to wait for the female, the hen, to lay eggs.

b.) Courtship Behavior in Finches

In addition to learning how to differentiate between the males and females of different finch species, you should also familiarize yourself with courtship behavior. During breeding season, males of the species often become more active and aggressive. In captivity, the male will exhibit certain courtship behaviors in an attempt to attract the attention of the female. For example, the male might sing to the female or engage in a sort of dance involving some of the following movements: standing tall, bowing, puffing out the feathers, hopping up and down, holding a blade of grass, pointing the tail, shaking the head, or brushing the beak against a perch.

If the female is receptive to the male's advances, the two will form a pair bond. Some signs that indicate the formation of a pair bond in finches include sleeping or perching side by side, grooming or preening each other, calling or cooing to each other, and building a nest together. In some species, these signs may be more pronounced than in others. For example, some species like the zebra finch prefer to be in close physical contact with their mates while other species, like the Gouldian finch, may simply tolerate the presence of its mate, sitting near but not touching the other on the same perch.

c.) Nest Building in Finches

Once a male and a female finch form a pair bond, they will begin building a nest together. Most species of finches will accept an artificial nest box or a small basket, but some species prefer to build their own nests from raw materials. For finches that prefer to build their own nests, make sure to provide some of the following materials: strips of burlap, coconut fiber, shredded newspaper, shredded tissue. Do not give your finches yarn, hay, or hair to use for nesting material because these materials may be contaminated.

In most cases, your finches will begin building a nest on their own. If your finches do not seem interested in building a nest, you can encourage them to do so by placing a light near the entrance to the nest box or basket. If this still doesn't work, try providing another nest box or basket in a different location. Some finches even exhibit the opposite problem – overbuilding their nests. Just keep an eye on your finches as they build their nest to make sure that it isn't stuffed so full that the eggs or chicks will fall out of the nest box or basket.

2.) *The Breeding Process*

The actual breeding process for finches is unique from other animals because neither sex has any external genitalia. The sex organs of both male and female finches are located internally, accessible via the cloaca. The opening of the cloaca is called the "vent" and it can be found on the underside of the body, just where the tail joins the body of the bird. For successful copulation to occur between a male and female finch, the male must touch his cloaca to hers, thus enabling the transfer of his ejaculate to her sex organs. This process is referred to as the "cloacal kiss."

In order for the male to press his cloaca to the female's, the hen typically lifts her tail and the male presses his body against hers, placing one leg over her back. The male usually flaps his wings frantically to help keep his body pressed against hers and the whole process usually only lasts for a few seconds. Some species of finch will mate out in the open, like the zebra finch, while others prefer to mate inside the nesting box, like the Gouldian finch. After a successful copulation, the female finch can store the male's sperm inside the reproductive tract for several days and the pair may mate several times.

a.) Egg Laying Behavior

Female finches, or hens, typically lay their eggs during the early morning hours and they usually lay just one egg per day. Some of the signs your female finch may exhibit which indicate imminent egg laying may include decreased defecation, straining, or a wide-based stance. In most cases, you will not actually witness your finch laying her eggs because they will do so inside the nesting box and during the very early hours of the morning. The average clutch size for finches ranges from 1 to 9 eggs with 3 to 6 being the most common number. Hens can lay eggs even if they have not mated with a male, but the eggs will be infertile.

b.) Egg Incubation and Hatching

Once the hen lays her eggs she will incubate them by resting on top of them to keep them warm. Some finches do not begin incubating their eggs until the third or fourth egg has been laid, and some do not begin until all of the eggs have been laid from one clutch. Once the incubation period begins, it typically lasts between 12 and 16 days as long as the eggs are fertile. For most finch species, the male and female share the job of keeping the eggs incubated during the day but the hen typically incubates the eggs at night. In some cases, the cock may share the nest with the female at night, helping to incubate the eggs, or he may sleep elsewhere in the cage.

In some cases, finches may abandon their eggs and their nest. This may result from a number of factors including disturbances to the nest by humans (touching or moving the nest, making loud noises nearby, etc.); pests such as cockroaches or ants; nosey cage mates or loud noises nearby; or nighttime disturbances. While your finches are incubating their eggs, it is important that you disturb them as little as possible. Be very careful when changing food and water dishes and, if possible, position the dishes so they are accessible from outside the cage so you don't have to put your hands in the cage directly. Keep the area around the cage as quiet as possible during incubation as well.

3.) Raising the Babies

In most cases, your finches' eggs will hatch after 12 to 16 days of incubation. Once they do, the parents will care for the chicks, taking turns feeding them. Finch chicks are born blind and featherless, completely dependent upon their parents for warmth and food. During the first day or two after hatching the parents may not feed the chicks because they will still be absorbing the remainder of their yolk sac for energy. During this time the parents may still prod at the chicks and attempt to feed them.

After hatching, the parents will continue to incubate the hatchlings for about 10 days until their juvenile plumage begins to develop. After this point the parents may still incubate the hatchlings, but typically only at night. The chicks will not open their eyes until they are about 6 days old and they typically do not leave the nest until 14 to 20 days after hatching. Even when the chicks fledge, or leave the nest, they will still be dependent on the parents for some time yet.

To ensure that your finches keep their chicks properly fed you need to provide an assortment of high-quality foods. The parents will eat the food and then regurgitate it and feed it to their chicks. For most species of finch, the parents will feed the chicks for 4 to 6 weeks after which point they will become weaned, or begin feeding on their own. Most finch parents will naturally wean their chicks by feeding them less and less while encouraging them to eat food on their own.

Once you have witnessed each of the chicks eating and drinking on their own it is time to remove them to a separate cage, away from the parents. In some cases, the parents may be eager to breed again and they might start chasing the chicks out of the nest. Even if your finches are eager to breed again, you should limit their breeding to 2 or 3 clutches per year for their own wellbeing.

Chapter Seven: Keeping Finches Healthy

In addition to providing your finches with a safe, clean habitat and a healthy diet, you also need to look out for common diseases. Even if you take every precaution, your finches could still come down with an illness, so it is your job to learn as much as you can about common finch diseases so you know what to do when the time comes. In this chapter you will receive information about the most common diseases affecting finches including the symptoms, causes, and treatment options. You will also receive information about preventing disease to keep your finches happy and healthy.

1.) Common Health Problems

The best way to keep your finches healthy is to provide them with a safe, clean environment and a healthy diet. Even if you are extremely careful to provide for the basic needs of your finches, however, they are still prone to contracting certain diseases. <u>The most common diseases and conditions affecting finches are listed below</u>:

- Air Sac Mites
- Aspergillosis
- Coccidiosis
- Egg Binding
- Feather Mites/Lice
- Giardiasis
- Nutritional Deficiency
- Overgrown Claws
- Parasitical Worms
- Scaly Face

In the following pages you will receive detailed information about each of these diseases or conditions including symptoms, causes, treatment options and methods for prevention.

Air Sac Mites

This condition is most commonly seen in Gouldian finches and canaries and it can be a very dangerous, even fatal disease. Air sac mites, taxonomically classified as *Sternostoma tracheacolum*, affect the respiratory tract of infected birds. Common symptoms include coughing, abnormal chirp or song, and loss of voice. In many cases, the symptoms of air sac mites are difficult to identify which is why the disease often progresses to dangerous levels before it is even detected.

Air sac mites are most commonly transmitted from adult finches to their young during feeding cycles. Though it is possible for air sac mites to be transferred between adult birds, it is fairly rare. Treatment options for air sac mites include a topical insecticide spray containing Ivermectin to kill the mites in all stages of its life cycle. When treating for air sac mites it is important that you treat the entire flock, not just the birds that are known to be affected.

Aspergillosis

Aspergillosis is a type of respiratory infections which is caused by a fungus called *Aspergillus*. This fungus is naturally found in nearly every environment but it typically doesn't affect finches unless their immune systems are already weakened by stress, poor nutrition, injury, or another infection. Aspergillosis is especially common in flocks that are kept in cramped, crowded conditions. Prolonged use of certain medications like corticosteroids or antibiotics may also predispose finches to aspergillosis.

The most common signs of aspergillosis include rapid breathing, difficulty breathing, exercise intolerance, and a change in voice. Aspergillosis may be either acute or chronic with chronic aspergillosis being both more common and more deadly. In severe cases, the central nervous system of infected birds may become involved and symptoms like tremors, seizures and paralysis may present. Treatment options for aspergillosis may include antifungal medication – these may be administered orally, topically, or by injection. In severe cases, surgery may be required to remove lesions.

Coccidiosis

This disease is caused by a type of protozoan parasite known as Eimeria. These parasites develop and grow inside the intestinal tract of infected birds and, as they reproduce, they will cause swelling of the intestinal tissue and bleeding. Damage to the intestine often results in loss of liquid (dehydration) and problems with absorbing nutrients from food.

Unfortunately, the parasite responsible for coccidiosis is fairly common – it is very common in wild birds and can be found naturally in many domestic bird populations as well. Outbreaks of coccidiosis are most likely to occur during wet periods and it also tends to occur in cramped cages where conditions are poor.

In many cases, finches affected by coccidiosis do not show any symptoms until the infection has progressed and they become severely stressed. Common symptoms of coccidiosis include lethargy, weight loss, diarrhea, bloody stool, and dehydration. Treatment options include medication with an anti-parasitic – these treatments can often be administered in the birds' feed.

Egg Binding

Egg binding is a condition that affects female birds and it is a condition that is typically easy to identify. If your female bird is egg bound she will likely be lying on the floor of the cage, exhibiting obvious signs of distress. The finch may be straining to pass the egg and her feathers may be raised in distress – if she does not pass the egg, she will die. Unfortunately, there is not much you can do for a female finch who is already egg bound – trying to force her to pass the egg could result in fatal injury.

The best thing you can do for an egg bound female is to place her in a quarantine cage and monitor her closely. In some cases, adding cod liver oil to your finches' diet can help to prevent egg binding – making sure your finches get enough calcium will also help. Egg binding is most commonly seen during cold weather but it can affect birds at any time of year if their diet is lacking in calcium or certain oils.

Feather Mites/Lice

There are a number of different species of mites which can infect finches with lice, red mites, and chiggers being the most common. Lice are very difficult to spot with the naked eye and they tend to spend their entire life cycle on the bird, rarely passing from one bird to another. Lice can, however, be spread by fallen feathers. These parasites can survive for months while on the bird and they reproduce very quickly, laying large quantities of eggs that hatch in just a few days. Signs of lice in finches include restlessness, ruffling of feathers, excessive preening, and feather damage.

Red mites can also affect finches and they tend to make the bird restless, irritable, and itchy. These mites are nocturnal so you will only be able to see them at night, typically around the head or the vent area. Red mites are opportunistic parasites so they may travel from your birds to other pets, even humans. Chiggers are an immature stage of various types of mites and they tend to collect on the breast, thighs, underside, and near the vent of affected birds. Treatment options for feather mites and lice include medications like Permectrin 11 and Avian Insect Liquidator. You may need to continue treatment for several weeks to kill the mites or lice in all of their life stages.

Giardiasis

This disease is caused by a protozoan parasite that inhabits the small intestines of infected birds. The most common symptoms of giardiasis include diarrhea, malabsorption of nutrients, itching, and pulling at the feathers. In some cases, finches infected with giardiasis may develop dry, flaky skin. In cases that involve feather plucking, the areas most affected include the thighs, chest, and the underside of the bird's wings.

Giardiasis is somewhat difficult to diagnose because they are very fragile organisms and, though they are passed in the bird's droppings, they may disintegrate before a diagnosis can be made. A fecal exam is the best way to diagnose this condition and it can only be performed by a qualified veterinarian. Treatment options for giardiasis include anti-protozoal treatments like Ronivet. You may need to continue treatment for a week or more and, in some cases, the bird may never be completely cured of the disease.

Nutritional Deficiencies

Nutritional deficiencies can affect all species of finches and different deficiencies may produce different symptoms. There are two main causes for nutritional deficiencies: either there is a lack of a particular nutrient in the diet or there is an imbalance in the finch's diet. In cases where there is a lack of a certain nutrient in the diet, adding more of that particular nutrient will usual resolve symptoms and improve the bird's condition. If there is an imbalance of nutrients, particularly and overload of certain nutrients, the entire diet may need to be reformulated.

Signs of protein deficiencies may include weight loss, changes in plumage color, stress lines on the feathers, and poor feathering. A deficiency of fats in the diet produces similar symptoms with the addition of neurological abnormalities and reduced resistance to disease. Deficiencies in vitamin A can lead to gout, muted feather coloration, and the development of white pustules in the mouth, crop, and nasal passages. A deficiency of vitamin E may result in twitching, neurological abnormalities, and reproductive abnormalities.

If you suspect that your finches are suffering from a nutritional deficiency you can try adding more of the nutrient in question to their diet – you may also want to contact your veterinarian for advice. Be very careful when adding supplementary nutrients to your finch's diet because it is very easy to overload the diet with certain nutrients and this could lead to even more problems. Before you make any significant changes to your finches' diet, consult your veterinarian and then make the changes very gradual so you do not upset your finches' stomachs.

Overgrown Claws

All species of finches are prone to developing overgrown claws. While this problem may not cause an immediate threat to your finches, it does put them at an increased risk for injury. If their claws are too long they could catch on objects in the cage which could result in broken toes or even a broken leg. This is particularly likely if you use wire netting around your cage – it is never recommended that you use mesh screen to enclose a finch cage for this reason.

You should check the length of your finches' claws frequently and trim them as needed. Some species of finch have claws that grow very slowly, like the zebra finch, so they seldom need to be trimmed. Other species like owl finches and society finches may require occasional trimming while strawberry finches, waxbills, and orange cheeks require frequent trimming. Be very careful when you are trimming your finches' claws to make sure that you do not cut the quick. Keep some styptic powder on hand when you are trimming claws just in case you cut one too short and you need to stop the bleeding.

Parasitical Worms

The most common way finches contract parasitical worms is through live feed such as mealworms and contaminated droppings. It is also possible for adult finches to pass them on to their young during feeding cycles. Finches that are kept in outdoor enclosures are also at risk for contracting parasitical worms from wild birds. Luckily, parasitical worms are fairly easy to diagnose – you will be able to see them in your finches' droppings. They may also be present in the bird's mouth and in food or water bowls.

There are many different types of parasitical worms including threadworms, tapeworms, caecal worms, roundworms, gizzard worms and gape worms. Treatment options for parasitical worms typical involve medication with some kind of anti-parasitic or a broad-spectrum dewormer that contains either Praziquantel or Levamisole. These anti-parasitics will cover all of the worms that are known to affect finches. Dosing instructions will vary from one medication to another, so be sure to read the label and follow the directions carefully.

Scaly Face

Scaly face is a problem that commonly affects society finches and other species. This condition is actually cause by a type of mite that feeds on the outer layers of the skin on the bird's face and then burrows into the skin to lay its eggs. When the eggs hatch and the mites begin to grow, it causes a scaly appearance to form on the face, particularly around the beak. The infestation causes localized swelling of the tissues around the beak as well as pitting and the formation of lesions. In the case of severe infestations, the finch may be permanently disfigured.

The most common method of transmission for scaly mites occurs in the nest box during periods of feeding – it is very easy for parent finches to pass the mites on to their young. Transmission between adult finches is possible, but it is much less likely. Treatment options vary depending on the severity of the disease. In many cases, a topical treatment with paraffin is sufficient to resolve the infestation. In cases where only the upper mandible is affected, this treatment should be performed daily or twice daily for two to four weeks until the infestation is resolved. Just make sure that the bird doesn't swallow the paraffin because it could cause diarrhea which could lead to dehydration.

2.) Preventing Illness

One of the most dangerous mistakes you can make when keeping pet finches is allowing your finches to become exposed to toxic plants. Many finch owners like to use live plants as decorations in their finch cage but, unless you are sure that the plant is non-toxic to finches, you shouldn't use it. <u>The following plants are considered toxic for finches</u>:

- Avocado
- Clematis
- Oleander
- Poinsettia
- Yew
- Bishop's weed

- Burdock root
- Castor bean
- Dieffenbachia
- Ergot
- Maternity plant
- Nightshade

- Parsley
- Black locust
- Lily of the valley
- Philodendron
- Rhododendron
- Virginia creeper

- Camel bush
- Coffee bean
- Locoweed
- Milkweed
- Oak
- Tobacco

The following plants are considered generally safe for use around finches:

- Bougainvillea
- Dogwood
- Tiger lily
- Boston fern
- Marigold
- Magnolia
- Gardenia
- Hibiscus

- Dandelion
- Petunia
- Baby's breath
- Bird's nest fern
- Creeping fig
- Fountain grass
- Umbrella tree

In addition to making sure that your finches do not come into contact with any dangerous plants, you also need to careful to keep their cage clean and disinfected. Clean, disinfect and refill your bird's water bowl on a daily basis and keep the food bowls clean as well. You should also plan to clean small enclosures once a week and disinfect them on a monthly basis. For very large enclosures, clean the floor once a week, scrub the enclosure every two weeks, and disinfect the cage once a month.

<u>When cleaning and disinfecting your finch cage, follow the procedure outlined below</u>:

1. Remove all of the birds to a separate enclosure – the separate enclosure should be spaced well away with a separate air source so your finches aren't affected by disinfectant fumes

2. Remove all toys and objects from the cage and clean them separately.

3. Create a solution using ¾ cup bleach per 1 gallon of water – this will create a 5% solution.

4. Scrub the cage well using only water and rinse everything to remove feces, food, bedding, and other contaminants.

5. Spray the 5% bleach solution onto the cage and soak all toys, dishes and accessories for a full 30 minutes.

6. Rinse the cage and all cage accessories well to remove all traces of the bleach solution and let them air dry before returning your birds to the cage.

3.) Quarantining/Introducing New Birds

When you bring home new finches to add to an already existing flock, you need to be very careful. Even if you are sure to evaluate your new finches before you buy them for signs of good health, they could still be carrying some kind of disease. When you introduce the new bird to your existing flock, then, that disease could spread rapidly and it could be devastating for your finches. The only way to prevent this from happening is to quarantine all new birds before you add them to your flock.

The proper procedure for quarantining new birds is to keep them in a separate cage well away from your existing flock for at least 6 to 8 weeks. If your new bird doesn't show any signs of illness during this period, it can be considered safe to add them to your flock. It is important to note that certain diseases that affect birds do not produce symptoms in carriers. Examples of these diseases include Paramyxovirus infection and giardiasis. In these cases, quarantine alone may not even be enough to identify the disease.

In addition to quarantining new birds, you should also have them examined by a veterinarian. During the quarantine period, you may also want to treat your new birds for common parasites and have stool samples collected and tested by your vet. Common parasites you could treat for include coccidian, giardia, mites, and worms. Do not use antibiotics as a preventive treatment because it could result in the bacteria that naturally live inside birds to build up a resistance which could then result in an infection.

Once your new birds have been quarantined and cleared by your vet, you can add them to your existing cage. The best way to do this without causing your existing flock to become territorial is to remove all of the birds from the cage and then completely rearrange it. Then, add all of the birds (including your new finches) back to the cage at the same time. Monitor your birds for a few days to make sure that they are getting along. If your existing flock bullies the new birds or rejects them completely, you may need to house them separately.

Chapter Eight: Finches Care Sheet

In reading this book you have received a vast amount of information about finches in general as well as tips for their care. When you bring your own finches home and begin to care for them, you may find that you have questions or that you need to reference specific pieces of information from this book. To save you the hassle of flipping through the entire book to find a small nugget of information, all of the most important details about finches and their care have been gathered in this chapter to provide you with a handy care sheet. Here you will find all of the key information about finches as well as their habitat, diet, and breeding.

1.) Basic Information

- **Classification**: most finches belong to the order
  Passeriformes or Estrildidae
- **Taxonomy**: passerine finches are referred to as "true
  finches" while finches in the Estrildidae family are
  called waxbills or estrildid finches
- **Distribution**: most finches are found in the Northern
  Hemisphere while estrildid finches are found in the
  Old World tropics and Australia
- **Habitat**: typically found in grasslands or wooded
  areas, though some species inhabit mountainous or
  desert regions
- **Anatomical Adaptations**: finches have four toes on
  each foot (three toes facing forward, one backward);
  finches have a unique ability to perch on vertical
  surfaces and they can remain perched while sleeping
  without falling off
- **Eggs**: passerine finches lay colored eggs with 2 to 5
  average per clutch
- **Hatchling**: passerine finches are born blind and
  featherless; finch chicks require a great deal of parental
  care
- **Physical Characteristics**: large, often stubby beaks; flat
  head; short wings
- **Coloration**: brown (often with a green tinge) is
  common; black is commonly seen on the wings and

tail with white plumage largely absent except in wing bars; males often exhibit bright red or yellow coloration

- **Sexual Dimorphism**: females often lack the bright colorings seen on males of many species
- **Diet**: primarily granivorous (eating seeds), though some species eat berries and small arthropods (insects)
- **Vocalization**: most finches sing with some species being very loud and boisterous; each species has a unique vocalization with individual birds having their own song
- **Flight Pattern**: bouncing pattern alternating between periods of flapping with periods of gliding on closed wings
- **Lifespan**: average 4 to 7 years

2.) *Cage Set-up Guide*

- **Minimum Cage Dimensions**: 18 by 24 inches (45.7 by 61 cm) for two finches
- **Minimum Floor Space**: 3 to 4 square feet (0.9 to 1.2 square meters) per bird
- **Minimum Height**: 16 inches(40.6 cm); higher for larger cages/more finches
- **Required Accessories**: food and water dish, perches, toys, nests, nesting materials
- **Food/Water Dish**: best material is stainless steel; plastic or glass are second best
- **Positioning Dishes**: place food and water dishes on opposite sides of the cage
- **Perches**: several throughout the cage at different heights; best material is clean hardwood
- **Recommended Toys**: swing, ropes, ladders, etc.
- **Materials to Avoid**: yarn or small synthetic fibers (finches could choke on them)
- **Additional Decorations**: silk plants or live non-toxic plants
- **Nests**: wooden nest box (will need to be replaced occasionally); plastic or metal box (clean and disinfect occasionally); nest basket
- **Nesting Materials**: strips of burlap, coconut fiber, shredded newspaper, shredded tissue

- **Materials for Homemade Cage**: industrial-grade epoxy paint, exterior-grade plywood, PVC powder-coated galvanized wire, and all-plastic hardware netting
- **Lighting**: natural, direct sunlight or a light from a full-spectrum bulb which mimics natural sunlight
- **Artificial Lighting**: plug into an automatic timer that will turn them on at sunrise and off at sunset
- **Recommended Temperature Range**: between 70°F and 80°F (21° to 27°C)
- **Humidity Level**: between 50% and 70%; depends on natural habitat of particular species
- **Adjusting Humidity**: add a bird bath or mist the cage occasionally with clean water

3.) Nutritional Information

- **Diet in the Wild**: primarily seeds, some berries and arthropods (insects)
- **Diet in Captivity**: seed mix supplemented with fresh greens, eggs, and cuttlebone
- **Nutritional Needs**: protein, carbohydrate, fat, vitamins, minerals, and fresh water
- **Protein**: ten essential amino acids; promotes healthy bone, feather, and muscle production; back-up energy source
- **Carbohydrate**: primary energy source; deficiencies can result in neurological problems
- **Fats**: supports production of cells and membranes; some fats used for energy; too much fat can interfere with nutrient absorption
- **Fat-Soluble Vitamins**: can be stored longer than water-soluble; most important are vitamin D3, vitamin E, vitamin A, and vitamin K
- **Water-Soluble Vitamins**: most important are riboflavin, niacin, thiamin, biotin, pantothenic acid, vitamin B12, vitamin C, pyridoxine, and choline
- **Minerals**: support bone growth, muscle function and egg production; most important are phosphorus, calcium, magnesium, copper, iron, selenium, zinc, iodine, sodium, manganese, and chlorine

- **Recommended Diet Structure**: 70% commercial finch diet, 30% supplementary foods
- **Best Seeds to Feed**: Canary grass seed, White millet, Plate millet, Panicum millet, Japanese millet, Niger seed
- **Supplementary Foods**: kale, lettuce, spinach, dandelion greens, carrot tops, apples, pears, sprouted seeds, eggs, cuttlebone
- **Feeding Amount**: 1 to 2 teaspoons seed per day; supplemental foods in very small portions
- **Feeding Tips**: rotate supplemental foods for variety; freeze seed mixes for 7 days to kill moth/beetle larvae

4.) Breeding Tips

- **Sexual Dimorphism**: some species exhibit physical differences between males and females that can be observed visually (ex: Gouldian finch and cordon bleu waxbill)
- **Colors/Mutation**: some color variants or mutations may not exhibit physical differences (ex: white zebra finch)
- **Seasonal Changes**: some sexually dimorphic species only exhibit changes during breeding season (ex: strawberry finch)
- **Sexual Monomorphism**: in some species, males and females look the same even during breeding season (ex: society finch)
- **Sexual Differentiation**: in sexually monomorphic species, the sexes can be differentiated by differences in song or by the female laying eggs
- **Courtship Behavior**: male becomes more active and aggressive; courts female with song and dance
- **Pair Bond:** if the female accepts the male's advances, they form a pair bond
- **Signs of Pair Bonding**: sleeping or perching side by side, grooming or preening each other, calling or cooing to each other, and building a nest together
- **Recommended Nesting Materials**: strips of burlap, coconut fiber, shredded newspaper, shredded tissue

- **Materials to Avoid**: yarn, corn cob, leaves, soil, eucalyptus, hay, or hair
- **Sexual Anatomy**: no external genitalia; sex organs of both male and female finches are located internally
- **Copulation**: male and female touch their cloacas together so the male can transfer his ejaculate - the "cloacal kiss"
- **Egg Laying**: females typically lay one egg per day in the early morning
- **Clutch Size**: ranges from 1 to 9 eggs with 3 to 6 being the most common
- **Incubation Period**: typically lasts from 12 to 16 days with male and female sharing the responsibility
- **Hatching**: chicks hatch after 12 to 16 days; chicks emerge blind, featherless, and completely helpless
- **Raising Chicks**: hatchlings are incubated for another 10 days; eyes open at 6 days
- **Fledging**: chicks begin to leave the nest after 14 to 20 days but are still dependent on parents for feeding
- **Weaning**: most finches feed their chicks for 4 to 6 weeks then naturally begin feeding them less and less while encouraging them to eat on their own
- **Breeding Frequency**: pairs may be eager to breed again; limit breeding to 2 or 3 clutches per year

Chapter Nine: Relevant Websites

When you are preparing your home for your finches, there are many things you will need to shop for including a cage, cage decorations/toys, and food. You may also want to do a little extra research on your own to make sure that you have a good understanding of finches before you buy them. In this chapter you will find lists of relevant websites to help you in your quest for the perfect cage as well as resources for cage decorations, food and accessories. You will also find a list of resources for more detailed information about finches and their care.

1.) Food for Finches

Below you will find a list of relevant websites about food for finches – this includes not only suppliers of finch food but feeding tips as well.

United States Websites:

"Diet and Nutrition." Finch Information Center. <http://www.finchinfo.com/diet/index.php>

"The Best Canary and Finch Food." AllPetBirds.com. <http://www.all-pet-birds.com/finch-food.html>

"Finch/Canary Food." Drs. Foster and Smith. <http://www.drsfostersmith.com/bird-supplies/food-formulas-diets/finch-canary-food-diets/ps/c/5059/5911/5912>

"Finches – Feeding." VCA Animal Hospitals. <http://www.vcahospitals.com/main/pet-health-information/article/animal-health/finches-feeding/867>

"Bird Food, from Pellets to Seeds." PetSolutions. <http://www.petsolutions.com/C/Pet-Bird-Food.aspx>

United Kingdom Websites:

"Feeding Zebra Finches." The Zebra Finch Society.
<http://www.zebrafinchsociety.co.uk/index.php?option=co
m_content&view=article&id=42:feeding-zebra-
finches&catid=15:zebra-finches&Itemid=64>

"Bird Food and Treats." Pet-Supermarket.co.uk.
<http://www.pet-supermarket.co.uk/Category/
Caged_Bird_Supplies-Bird_Food_Treats>

"Pet Bird Food." Cages World.
<http://www.cagesworld.co.uk/c/Pet_Bird_Food.htm>

"Bird Seeds." Seapets.co.uk. <http://www.seapets.co.uk/
products/bird-supplies/bird-food/bird-seeds/>

"Seed and Feed." Cagefronts.co.uk.
<http://www.cagefronts.co.uk/seed-feed.html#/page/1>

"Bird Snacks and Crackers." Zooplus.co.uk.
<http://www.zooplus.co.uk/shop/birds/snacks_and_supple
ments>

"Seed Bearing Plants for Attracting Wild Finches." The
Garden of Eaden. <http://gardenofeaden.blogspot.co.uk/
2009/08/seed-bearing-plants-for-attracting-wild.html>

2.) Cages for Finches

Below you will find a list of relevant websites about cages for finches – this includes not only websites for purchasing cages but tips for housing finches as well.

United States Websites:

"Housing and Environment." Finch Information Center. <http://www.finchinfo.com/housing/index.php>

"Canary and Finch Cages." That Pet Place. <http://www.thatpetplace.com/pet-supplies-search#!bird-supplies/bird-cages&ea_c=canary-finch-cages>

"Finch Bird Cages." BirdCages4Less. <http://birdcages4less.com/page/B/CTGY/Finch-Bird-Cages>

"Cages for Small Birds." Drs. Foster and Smith. <http://www.drsfostersmith.com/bird-supplies/bird-cages-aviaries/small-bird-cages/ps/c/5059/10346/5062>

"Small Bird Cages for Canaries, Finches and Parakeets." PetSolutions. <http://www.petsolutions.com/C/Small-Bird-Cages-Canaries-Finches-Parakeets+SAll.aspx>

United Kingdom Websites:

"Bird Cages and Stands." Pet-Supermarket.co.uk.
<http://www.pet-supermarket.co.uk/Category/
Caged_Bird_Supplies-Bird_Cages_Stands>

"Finch Cages." Amazon.co.uk.
<http://www.amazon.co.uk/s/ref=nb_sb_noss?url=search-
alias%3Dpets&field-keywords=finch+cage&rh=n%
3A340840031%2Ck%3Afinch+cage>

"Finch Bird Cages." Cages World.
<http://www.cagesworld.co.uk/c/Finch_Bird_Cages.htm>

"Bird Cages." Zooplus.co.uk.
<http://www.zooplus.co.uk/shop/birds/bird_cages_and_acc
essories>

"Budgie Cages, Canary and Finch Cages." Seapets.co.uk.
<http://www.seapets.co.uk/products/bird-supplies/bird-
cages/budgie-cages-canary-and-finch-cages/>

3.) Toys and Accessories for Finches

Below you will find a list of relevant websites about toys and accessories for finches – this includes not only suppliers of these items but tips for decorating your cage as well.

United States Websites:

"Bird Cage Accessories." That Pet Place. <http://www.thatpetplace.com/pet-supplies-search#!bird-supplies&ea_c=bird-cage-accessories>

"Bird Perches, Swings and Playlands." PetSolutions. <http://www.petsolutions.com/C/Bird-Perches-Swings-Playlands.aspx>

"Finch Toys." Pet Mountain. <http://www.petmountain.com/category/1012/1/finch-toys.html>

"Finches Toys." Petco.com. <http://www.petco.com/N_56_101/Finch-Toys.aspx>

"What Sorts of Toys Can I Make for My Pet Finches." The Nest Pets. <http://pets.thenest.com/sorts-toys-can-make-pet-finches-6651.html>

United Kingdom Websites:

"Bird Swings, Perches and Ladders." Pet-Supermarket.co.uk. <http://www.pet-supermarket.co.uk/Category/Caged_Bird_Supplies-Bird_Swings_Perches_Ladders>

"Bird Baths." Supapets-online.co.uk. <http://www.supapets-online.co.uk/bird-baths/>

"Nests, Nesting and Bedding." Cagefronts.co.uk. <http://www.cagefronts.co.uk/accessories.html?cat=43>

"Bird Cages and Accessories." Amazon.co.uk. <http://www.amazon.co.uk/birdcages-accessories/b?ie=UTF8&node=471265031>

"Bird Cage Accessories." Zooplus.co.uk. <http://www.zooplus.co.uk/shop/birds/cage_accessories>

"Bird Cage Accessories." Cages World. <http://www.cagesworld.co.uk/c/Bird_Cage_Accessories.htm>

4.) General Info for Finches

Below you will find a list of relevant websites about general information for finches – this includes information about popular species and other info you might find helpful.

United States Websites:

"Try a Finch as a Pet Bird." Bird Channel. <http://www.birdchannel.com/bird-species/find-the-right-bird/try-a-finch.aspx>

"Finches Species Profile." That Pet Place. <http://www.thatpetplace.com/finches-article>

"Bird Care Guide: Finch." MSPCA Education. <http://www.mspca.org/programs/pet-owner-resources/pet-owner-guides/bird-care-adoption/bird-care-guide-finch.pdf>

"Finch." Lafeber Company. <http://lafeber.com/pet-birds/species/finch/>

"Caring for Finches: An Expert Guide by Pets Adviser." Pets Adviser. <http://www.petsadviser.com/misc/caring-for-finches-guide/>

United Kingdom Websites:

"Keeping Zebra Finches as Pets." Pets World.
<http://www.petsworld.co.uk/zebrafinches.htm>

"Bengalese Finch." The Society for Conservation in
Aviculture. < http://www.thesca.org.uk/bird-
care/bengalese-finch>

"Finch Care." Superpet Warehouse.
<http://www.superpetwarehouse.co.uk/finch-care.html>

"Birds." The Royal Society for the Prevention of Cruelty to
Animals. <https://www.rspcansw.org.au/animals/birds>

"Keeping Canaries as Pets." Pets World.
<http://www.petsworld.co.uk/canaries.htm>

Index

D

E

F

G

H

I

L

M

male · 5, 77, 78, 79, 80, 81, 83, 84, 85, 113, 114, 132
mandibles · 3
Migratory Bird Treaty Act · 36, 140
minerals · 68, 70, 72, 111
molt · 65
monthly costs · 43

N

nail clippers · 44
nails · 44, 73, 75, 76
nares · 57
natural selection · 15
nest · 4, 43, 44, 63, 80, 81, 85, 87, 100, 102, 109, 113, 114, 135
nest box · 63, 81, 82, 100, 109
nesting · 5, 62, 63, 71, 77, 81, 84, 109
nesting material · 63, 77, 81
neurological · 69, 96, 111
nutrients · 69, 96, 97
nutritional deficiencies · 68, 96
nutritional needs · 68, 70

O

offspring · 3, 4
order · 5, 7, 11, 13, 14, 38, 47, 76, 83, 107
Overgrown Claws · 89, 98

P

pair bond · 80
parasites · 104
Parasitical Worms · 99
parental care · 8, 12, 107
parrots · 1, 42, 49, 60, 73, 76
Passeriformes · 7, 11, 13, 107
passerine · 7, 8, 11, 12, 13, 53, 107

Q

R

S

sick · 57

size · 8, 15, 40, 41, 42, 44, 49, 72, 84, 139

social · 3, 1, 40, 41, 60, 61

society finch · 16, 79, 113

song · 11, 12, 79, 108, 113

species · 2, 4, 5, 6, 7, 9, 10, 11, 12, 13, 14, 15, 16, 35, 36, 37, 38, 41, 42, 43, 49, 50, 51, 52, 60, 66, 67, 68, 71, 75, 78, 79, 80, 81, 84, 85, 87, 96, 98, 100, 107, 108, 110, 113, 122, 139

sperm · 3, 84

star finch · 16, 41

strawberry finch · 79, 113

stress · 58, 96

Strigiformes · 7

styptic powder · 75, 98

sunlight · 65, 110

supplemental diet · 67

supplier · 39, 50

swing · 63, 109

symptoms · 88, 89, 96, 104

T

tail · 4, 5, 10, 12, 42, 80, 83, 108

taming · 59, 76

temperament · 42, 58

temperature · 63, 64, 65, 139

toes · 7, 11, 75, 76, 98, 107

toys · 43, 44, 62, 63, 75, 103, 109, 115, 120

training · 59, 73

treatment · 88, 89, 100, 105

trimming · 44, 75, 98

true finches · 7, 9, 10, 11, 14, 107

V

vaccinations · 47

veterinary · 45, 47

vitamin D3 · 65, 70, 111

vitamins · 68, 69, 111

vocalizations · 10

W

water · 10, 44, 62, 66, 68, 69, 85, 102, 103, 109, 110, 111
waxbill · 7, 41, 78, 113
weaned · 58, 87
webbing · 8
wing · 3, 4, 5, 10, 12, 43, 44, 108
wings · 10, 12, 44, 73, 75, 76, 84, 107, 108
wren · 13

Z

zebra finch · 2, 10, 16, 78, 80, 84, 98, 113

Photo Credits

Cover Photo By Nigel Jacques via Wikimedia Commons, <http://en.wikipedia.org/wiki/Gouldian_finch#/media/File: GouldianFinches.jpg>

Page 1 Photo By Sandra via Wikimedia Commons, <http://en.wikipedia.org/wiki/Citril_finch#/media/File:Card uelis_citrinella_-Plateau_de_Beille,_Ariege,_Midi-Pyrenee,_France-8_(1).jpg>

Page 6 Photo By DickDaniels via Wikimedia Commons, <http://commons.wikimedia.org/wiki/File:House_Finch_R WD2012.jpg>

Page 9 Photo By Cephas via Wikimedia Commons, <http://en.wikipedia.org/wiki/File:Carpodacus_purpureus_ CT3.jpg>

Page 17 Photo By Martin Pot via Wikimedia Commons, <http://en.wikipedia.org/wiki/Gouldian_finch#/media/File: Male_adult_Gouldian_Finch.jpg>

Page 19 Photo By DickDaniels via Wikimedia Commons, <http://commons.wikimedia.org/wiki/File:Star_Finch_RWD. jpg>

Page 21 Photo By Gallo71 via Wikimedia Commons, <http://commons.wikimedia.org/wiki/File:Rbruni.JPG>

Page 23 Photo By Keith Gerstung via Wikimedia Commons, <http://en.wikipedia.org/wiki/Zebra_finch#/media/File:Taen iopygia_guttata_-Bird_Kingdom,_Niagara_Falls,_Ontario,_ Canada_-pair-8a.jpg>

Page 25 Photo By Dawn Huczek via Wikimedia Commons, <http://commons.wikimedia.org/wiki/File:A_Purple_Finch_ VS_House_Finch%3F_(3773173971).jpg>

Page 27 Photo By Nigel via Wikimedia Commons, <http://commons.wikimedia.org/wiki/File:House_Finch_426 8-002.jpg>

Page 31 Photo By Mdf via Wikimedia Commons, <http://en.wikipedia.org/wiki/List_of_birds_of_Iowa#/medi a/File:Carduelis-tristis-001.jpg>

Page 31 Photo By Adam Kumiszcza via Wikimedia Commons,
<http://commons.wikimedia.org/wiki/File:Carpodacus_eryt
hrinus_20060623.jpg>

Page 33 Photo By Jacob Spinks via Wikimedia Commons,
<http://commons.wikimedia.org/wiki/File:Green_Finch_(13
269570155).jpg>

Page 35 Photo By Flickr user Hazel Motes,
<https://www.flickr.com/photos/greg_scales/6288135694/siz
es/l>

Page 40 Photo By Ken Thomas via Wikimedia Commons,
<http://en.wikipedia.org/wiki/American_goldfinch#/media/
File:American_Goldfinch-27527.jpg>

Page 48 Photo By Danamania via Wikimedia Commons,
<http://en.wikipedia.org/wiki/Gouldian_finch#/media/File:
Young-gouldian-finch.jpg>

Page 50 Photo By Gil Dekel via Wikimedia Commons,
<http://en.wikipedia.org/wiki/Zebra_finch#/media/File:Zebr
a-Finch-at-Les-Bigoussies-France-Aug2010-by-Gil-
Dekel.jpg>

Page 54 Photo By Hansbirds via Wikimedia Commons, <http://commons.wikimedia.org/wiki/File:Red-browed_Finch_0065_Px1600.jpg>

Page 59 Photo By Ron Knight via Wikimedia Commons, <http://commons.wikimedia.org/wiki/File:Bright-rumped_Yellow-Finch_(8077601983).jpg>

Page 67 Photo By Flickr user Keith Ellwood, <https://www.flickr.com/photos/76377775@N05/6815690310/sizes/l>

Page 73 Photo By Peter Wilton via Wikimedia Commons, <http://commons.wikimedia.org/wiki/File:American_Goldfinch_(6973814398).jpg>

Page 77 Photo By Martin Pot via Wikimedia Commons, <http://en.wikipedia.org/wiki/Zebra_finch#/media/File:Zebrafinchchicks.jpg>

Page 81 Photo By Flickr user Wwarby, https://www.flickr.com/photos/wwarby/1584828743/sizes/l>

Page 83 Photo By Glen Fergus via Wikimedia Commons, <http://en.wikipedia.org/wiki/Red-browed_finch#/media/File:Red-browed_finch_mating.jpg

Page 86 Photo By Kelly Teague via Wikimedia Commons, <http://en.wikipedia.org/wiki/House_finch#/media/File:Car podacus_mexicanus_in_nest.jpg>

Page 88 Photo By Magnus Manske via Wikimedia Commons, <http://commons.wikimedia.org/wiki/ File:Zebra_finches_(7381576302).jpg>

Page 101 Photo By Francis C. Franklin via Wikimedia Commons, <http://en.wikipedia.org/wiki/Finch#/ media/File:Carduelis_carduelis_close_up.jpg>

Page 106 Photo By Gamweb via Wikimedia Commons, <http://commons.wikimedia.org/wiki/File:Snow_birds_finc hes_(404876688).jpg>

Page 115 Photo By Dominic Sherony via Wikimedia Commons, <http://commons.wikimedia.org/wiki/ File:Grassland_Yellow-finch_(Sicalis_luteola)_ (4089369507).jpg>

References

"A List of the Orders of the Class Aves: Birds." Earthlife.net.
<http://www.earthlife.net/birds/orders.html>

"Bird Terminology." Birds of North America. <http://www.birds-of-north-america.net/Bird_Terminology.html>

"Birds You Don't Need a License to Keep." Office of
Environment and Heritage.
<http://www.environment.nsw.gov.au/wildlifelicences/Birds
YouDontNeedALicenceToKeep.htm>

"Breeding Behaviors." Finch Information Center.
<http://www.finchinfo.com/breeding/behaviors.php>

"Breeding Finches." LadyGouldianFinch.com.
<http://www.ladygouldianfinch.com/features_breeding-myra.php>

"Catching and Handling Techniques." Finch Information Center.
<http://www.finchinfo.com/general/catching_and_handling.php>

"Choosing a Healthy Bird." About Home.
<http://birds.about.com/od/adoptingabird/a/babybirds.htm>

"Cost of Owning a Bird: Setup, Supplies, and Veterinary Care."
PetEducation.com. <http://www.peteducation.com/
article.cfm?c=15+1794&aid=1516>

"Finches – Feeding." VCA Animal Hospitals.
    <http://www.vcahospitals.com/main/pet-health-
    information/article/animal-health/finches-feeding/867>

"House Finch." All About Birds. <http://www.allaboutbirds.org/
    guide/House_Finch/id>

"House Finch." Drs. Foster and Smith.com
    <http://www.drsfostersmith.com/pic/article.cfm?articleid=344

"How Many Birds will fit in Your Cage?" Finch Information
    Center. <http://www.finchinfo.com/housing/
    cage_size_calculator.php>

"How to Breed Zebra Finches." The White Finch Aviary.
    <https://lebeaupinson.wordpress.com/2013/05/15/new-article-
    how-to-breed-zebra-finches/>

"Ideal Lighting, Temperature and Humidity." Finch Information
    Center. <http://www.finchinfo.com/housing/lighting_
    temperature_humidity.php>

"Inspecting and Choosing a Healthy Bird." Psittacine Breeding &
    Research Farm. <http://www.parrotpro.com/inspect.php>

"Keeping the Flight/Aviary Clean." Finch Information Center.
    <http://www.finchinfo.com/housing/disinfectants.php>

Lieberman, Karl. "Try a Finch as a Pet Bird." BirdChannel.com.
    <http://www.birdchannel.com/bird-species/find-the-right-
    bird/try-a-finch.aspx>

"List of Migratory Bird Species Protected by the Migratory Bird Treaty Act as of December 2, 2013." U.S. Fish & Wildlife Service Migratory Bird Program. <http://www.fws.gov/migratorybirds/RegulationsPolicies/mbta/MBTANDX.HTML

"Nail Clipping." Finch Aviary. <http://www.finchaviary.com/Maintenance/NailClipping.htm>

"Permits." U.S. Fish & Wildlife Service Migratory Bird Program. <http://www.fws.gov/migratorybirds/mbpermits.html>

"Pros and Cons of Buying a Canary or Other Pet Finch." Students with Birds. <https://studentswithbirds.wordpress.com/2013/12/22/pros-and-cons-of-buying-a-canary-or-other-pet-finch/>

"Safe Plants and Toxic Plants." Finch Information Center. <http://www.finchinfo.com/housing/safe_and_toxic_plants.php>

"Seed Mixes and Formulated Diets." Finch Information Center. <http://www.finchinfo.com/diet/seed_mixes_and_formulated_diets.php>

"The Migratory Bird Treaty Act of 1918." Maryland Department of Natural Resources. <http://www.dnr.state.md.us/wildlife/Plants_Wildlife/MBirdTreatyAct.asp>

"Zebra Finch – Where to Buy." Zebra Finch Society. <http://www.zebrafinch-society.org/where-to-buy-a-zebra-finch.htm>

"Zebra Finch Diet." Zebra Finch Society.
<http://www.zebrafinch-society.org/zebra-finch-diet.htm>

CPSIA information can be obtained
at www.ICGtesting.com
Printed in the USA
BVOW11s1052050318
509334BV00005B/23/P